The

umm

factor

(what you need in order to succeed)

THE

UMM

factor

(what you need in order to succeed)

MADELEINE KAY

Published by:

Chrysalis Publishing
P.O. Box 675
Flat Rock, NC 28731

ISBN 13: 978-0-9715572-1-5
ISBN 10: 0-9715572-1-7

Published in The United States of America

DEDicaTioN

To my son, Daniel Sage,
whom I love dearly and who inspires and grounds me.

To my mother, Anne Kay,
who is so gracious, kind, loving, beautiful and radiant
that she glows . . . and shows me how exquisite love is.

And to my dear friend Thea Patton Rosmini,
who helped me discover who I am
and the value of that.

And to my wonderful friend Federico Velludo,
who has been with me during the entire journey.

Thank you . . . each one of you.

ALSO BY MADELEINE KAY

Living Serendipitously . . . keeping the wonder alive
www.livingserendipitously.com

Living with Outrageous Joy
www.madeleinekay.com

Serendipitously Rich . . .
How to Get Delightfully, Delectably, Deliciously Rich
(or anything else you want) in 7 <u>Ridiculously</u> Easy Steps
www.serendipitouslyrich.com

The 7 Secrets to Living with Joy and Riches
www.madeleinekay.com

The 12 Myths About Money
www.madeleinekay.com

Coming Soon

Internet Success . . . 12 Secrets Revealed
www.madeleinekay.com

How Will I Ever Get Over My Happy Childhood
(Stories)
www.madeleinekay.com

CONTENTS

fOREWORD

I was totally blown away by the simple truth of this book . . . it drills down to the core . . . and reveals the nucleus of the secret power of your success . . . it's your *UMM* Factor.

What is your *UMM* Factor?

I don't want to give it away in this foreword, but I do want to motivate and inspire you to read all about it. Really learn it, believe in it, and then make a really solid irrevocable decision to put it into practice. Finally . . . just begin.

Here's a proactive way to guarantee your success right from the start. Take the smallest and most simple step . . . write your *UMM* Factor down. It can be on a 3x5 card, a napkin, or your journal . . . it doesn't matter, so long as you memorialize it in writing.

This one small action step will trigger an avalanche of effort from the universe, from your friends, and most importantly, from your own inner subconscious mind.

Madeleine Kay has a way of revealing profound wisdom in delightfully fun and fresh ways, so I highly recommend you read this book as fast as you can. Then read it again (and again) until you are absolutely certain that you know everything there is to know about your own *UMM* Factor.

DrProactive Randy Gilbert
President, Inside Success Productions, LLC

INTRODUCTION

There are 3 things everyone must have in order to succeed. Without all three, it is possible to succeed, but not likely. With them – your success is guaranteed.

These 3 things are simple, but not easy. They can't be bought, yet they are more precious than anything you can buy. They can't be faked – only the real thing will work. They can't be borrowed or imitated – they must be genuinely yours. They must be authentic.

13

Without these 3 things – the road to success is long and hard and arduous . . . fraught with pitfalls that can often seem insurmountable. With them however, you find yourself accomplishing what you desire with effortless ease as your success beckons you . . . calls to you and reaches out to you.

Without these 3 things, everything you do to succeed seems and feels like work – a tedious task. With them – there is no distinction between work and play – because everything you do is suffused with joy, energy, vitality . . . and sparkles.

Neither money, nor privilege, nor brains, nor education gives one person the advantage over another in possessing these 3 magical things that can transform your life from the mundane to the enthralling, from uneventful to adventurous, from impoverished to splendidly rich.

What are these 3 magical things? I call them the *UMM* Factor. What is your *UMM* Factor? You need to know this in order to succeed.

1

THE U fACTOR

Wow! The moment I wrote that (yes, I still write everything longhand!) and said it out loud, I realized how absolutely metaphorical and literal it is at the same time.

The U Factor – the absolutely essential first key to unlocking the secret of your success – is all about *you*. Who you are, what you care about, what excites you and ignites your passion, what gets you pacing in the middle of the night so you can't sleep because you can't get it out of your mind, what courses . . . no, races . . . through your blood like what Dylan Thomas calls – *through the green fuse drives the flower* – what you care about so much, that you will do anything it takes to get it, make it happen, do it, be it, have it.

What is this mysterious U Factor that does not leave you alone until you listen . . . until you *do* something about it? It is *urgency . . . a sense of urgency.*

What is urgency? It is passion. It is anger. It is fear turned to desperation. It is a talent that won't leave you alone until you use it. It is all of these things . . . one of these things . . . any of these things – all at the same time or separately. Urgency is whatever drives you . . . whatever urges you to do something . . . do it now . . . and keep on doing it.

Don't stop. It's too important. It means too much. You have to do it . . . you cannot not do it – whatever *it* is.

Where does this urgency come from? It comes from deep inside you . . . It comes from being so fed up with one situation that the pain of not doing something becomes more than the fear of doing it . . . It comes from a situation beyond your control that you will do whatever it takes to change and achieve your desired outcome . . . It comes from who and what you are, from your deepest values rising to the surface, coming together with your deepest desires to give you the courage, the passion, the will . . . the *anything* and *everything* you need to do what you want to do.

URGENCY AND FEAR

Urgency is not the same thing as fear. Fear paralyzes you. Urgency mobilizes you. Fear saps your energy. Urgency energizes you. Fear has you thinking about can'ts and shouldn'ts and all the ways you can't do what you want to do. Urgency has you looking for and finding ways you *can* do it, *can* succeed, *can* get what you want. Fear is often vague and abstract. Urgency is very specific and concrete – it comes from something

17

so important to you that it catapults you beyond the fear, so you don't even think about it . . . you just *do* it.

I remember seeing the film *Cindarella Man*, watching Russell Crowe play the real life Depression-era prize-fighter James Braddock – a washed up boxer who makes a comeback late in life. Braddock enjoyed some moderate success early in life which made him cocky, arrogant and flippant; he'd fought his fights with bravado, for his ego, for glory and recognition . . . nothing more . . . nothing of any real value to him.

During the stark bleakness of the Depression however, he can't feed his children and is reduced to tears and shame as he dilutes the little milk his family has with water so his children will have something to drink. With hat in hand and tears in his eyes, he goes to his friends begging for twenty dollars so he can get his children (who he had to give up because he couldn't feed them) back into his home, his former pride reduced to desperation.

But when Braddock is later asked at a press conference why he is returning to fighting at his age . . . and why, after so many poor showings, does he think he can succeed this time, he replies, "Because this time, I know what I'm fighting for." And the reporter asks him, "And what is that?" And Crowe replies, "Milk."

Wow . . . that says it all. That is powerful. That is urgency. That is real. That is visceral. And that's what urgency is all about – something that is gut level compelling. Something that is so important to you, that there is no *if* you will do it . . . only *when* you will do it.

URGENCY AND DESPERATION

Desperation is not the same thing as fear . . . it is exaggerated fear, fear multiplied in intensity. And it is this increased intensity that often propels people over that threshold of immobility and paralysis that is sapping their energy, making it impossible for them to act, to do something . . . *anything* to change their lives.

It is this increased intensity that transforms their dull ache into a real pain – a pain from which they will do *anything* to get away. And then . . . at some point, the desire to get *away* from the pain magically transforms into an urgency to move *toward* something else. The desire *for* becomes stronger than the need to avoid. The *will* to do, be, or have becomes empowered, activated and energized so there is no longer any looking backward, no more glancing over your shoulder to see what might be coming . . . there is only forward movement towards what you want.

It is this intensity that transforms a vague avoidance fear that drains all motivation into a concrete, specific urge *for* something. It is this intensity that ignites the fire inside; eliminates all *what if's, how can I's, but then's* . . . It is this intensity that provides a jet propulsion fuel that literally catapults you out of your lethargy and into action.

I suppose that's why you often hear people say that someone had to hit rock bottom before they *did* something . . . and *that something* is usually what wound up changing their life . . . usually set them on some path they were too afraid to go down before, a path they didn't even know they wanted to go down before, didn't feel worthy of going down, were afraid they would lose whatever little they had if they went down this new path.

So while fear can be immobilizing, desperation can be a source of unbounded energy urging you forward . . . toward what you want.

A few years ago, my friend's daughter went out

to California after university to get into the film industry. She went out with no money and soon found herself broke, in debt, and then in major debt.

When she first went out there, she worried about if she would make it in the industry. As her financial situation worsened and then finally became downright scary, she no longer worried about that, she worried about not having enough money. When things became dire, she found herself no longer focusing on worrying about money, but rather, on what she needed to do to survive and make money. Her questions became, "How can I get money and a job?" rather than "How can I get out of debt?" (Notice where the emphasis is in this question . . . on debt!) She asked herself "What do I need to do?" and "Who do I need to see?" Rather than "Can I get a job?" Her hypothetical questions slipped away and were replaced by questions governed by determination.

So her desperation became a great source of energy for her . . . energy that created a real sense of urgency that propelled her into action. No thinking, no planning, no procrastinating, worrying or *angsting* (my own word!) . . . just doing.

Anything can be a source of urgency – shame, pride, love, compassion . . . as long as the source gets you looking forward, not backward . . . gets you caring about and focusing on what you *want* and not what you don't want . . . gets you moving toward what you desire, not away from what you wish to avoid or eliminate. Human beings are not physically constructed to be able to look in two directions at the same time – so you cannot be looking at what you don't want, what you want to avoid at the same time you are looking toward what you *do* want. You have to make a choice . . . you have to commit to what you want and proceed towards it.

I remember hearing Sylvester Stallone tell the story of how desperation forced him to finally finish his script for *Rocky*, that he had been dragging his feet on for ages. He was in what I call *the dull ache period of lethargy* – that point at which you know you want to do something, but you just can't muster up the energy to do what you need to do, so you drag your feet, living what Thoreau calls "a life of quiet desperation."

He was living in New York, an out of work actor, struggling with fear of rejection, fear of failure, fear of success, fear of hard work, fear of not being good enough . . . who knows what fears he was dealing with that were dis-empowering and de-energizing him, preventing him from doing what he wanted to do. He had no money, a wife who was pregnant, was living in a run-down, seedy neighborhood, the only place he could afford . . . and he looked grungy and unkempt.

One night, he decided to go to the neighborhood liquor store for a bottle of wine. "And when I walked into the store to buy the wine," Stallone says, "I saw the guy in the store looking at me funny and inching away from me.

I realized he was avoiding me. And then I realized . . ." Stallone pauses and adds, almost incredulously, ". . . that he was afraid of me."

That moment was so powerful for Stallone . . . the shame he felt at that moment was so painful that it suddenly became less painful for him to finish the script than it was for him not to . . . and he went back to his apartment, he said, and wrote furiously, non-stop for the next five or seven or fourteen days (I can't remember which) and finished the script.

Anais Nin, a fabulous Diarist living in expatriate Paris in the 1930's, wrote in her *Diary* "And the day came when the risk to remain tight in a bud was more painful than the risk it took to blossom."

A sense of urgency makes it easy to take the risk. A sense of urgency takes the risk *out of* risk and makes it instead – compelling, exhilarating, energizing, empowering, exciting . . . and effortless.

URgency aND Passion

Donald Trump writes, "Without passion you don't have energy and without energy you have nothing." *Passion is* energy . . . passion creates a sense of urgency . . . passion makes everything happen with effortless ease.

I recently read a novel about Hollywood, and in it, the author writes that power in Hollywood is not money, fame, chutzpah or connections . . . power in Hollywood is passion. With passion, you can make anything happen . . .

with passion you can get anything done . . . with passion you can get anyone to help you or work with you.

Passion has so much energy, so much power, so much force that it actually by-passes the brain and normal mental processes. With passion, you process everything faster – almost instantaneously . . . With passion, you find yourself working, creating, doing things at superhuman levels – things that normally take weeks or months, you do in a day.

Passion is better than any amphetamine or drug you can ever take to increase your productivity, your creativity, your level of performance and achievement. Passion is what makes you unstoppable and compelling. No one can say "no" to you, everyone wants to work with you or help you or just be near you . . . to be around you to sop up some of that highly infectious, deliciously passionate energy and vitality that you exude.

And the air around you becomes charged with urgency, with life, with an *aliveness* that just sets things in motion, activates things, magnetizes the whole world to you . . . to what you want . . . to what you care so much about . . . to what you are doing.

And suddenly all your fears, your lethargy, your indecision . . . everything melts away and you are all powerful and know that you *can* do this . . . that you *will* do it . . . that you have power – real power – power that comes from your authentic self . . . power that nobody and nothing can alter or diminish.

I have a friend who called me two days ago gushing with passion for the first time in her life. Riddled with guilt about so many things she did and didn't do in her life, in constant debt, saddled with a poor education, a highly dysfunctional and abusive family life and childhood, she never believed she was worth anything . . . never felt like she deserved to live well or be happy or rich. So she could never muster the energy to do anything; she remained stuck for most of her life mired in a dull, boring, never-changing (not really, the details changed, but the value and quality of her life didn't) day-to-day existence.

Just coming out of a recent second emotionally abusive relationship right on the heels of her previous one, she suddenly discovered something she is passionate about – and now, she is giggling, singing, talking to groups about this magical product she wants to bring to people. She is even . . . acting silly . . . and loving it! She has never done any of these things before in her entire life.

Now suddenly . . . this person for whom nothing was ever possible . . . for whom everything was a huge effort . . . for whom everything good was always for others, but never for herself . . . this friend said to me (just in the course of conversation, not even as a willful, set intention, but more as *a fait accompli*) – "By next year, I'm going to have a place away from here (she lives in south Florida) so I don't have to deal with this heat and congestion anymore. I'm going to have a place in the mountains where I can go in the summer and a place here for the winter."

Wow! I was speechless . . . I was flabbergasted . . . and I never for a moment doubted, that she will (not would, but *will*) have that. She's found her passion and she is now all-powerful and unstoppable.

"Life's too short," she said. "I want to live. For the first time in my life, I want to live." This person who was resigned to being and willing to be, one of "the walking dead" her entire life and never saw even the glimmer of any other possibility and when she did, could never find the energy to do anything about it . . . suddenly came alive. Alive with a passion . . . an energy . . . a sense of urgency that completely eliminate the *if* from what she is doing . . . so her success is guaranteed.

And then . . . this person who is now suffused with urgency and passion and energy . . . this person who has never had, nor expected to have anything more than barely enough money to live . . . this person whose friends were always people who were stuck, hopeless and had nothing, because she didn't believe she was good enough to associate with any rich people, any educated people, any successful people . . . said to me "I don't want to hang around those people anymore. I am making new friends. If I want to be successful, I have to start being with successful people". . . and then, for emphasis, she added, "Right!"with a giggle.

That, by the way, is one of the most basic principles of success – *If you want to be successful, go where successful people are; if you want to be rich, associate with rich people; if you want to be cultured and sophisticated, frequent places the cultured and sophisticated do.* Without ever reading it, without ever learning it, without ever hearing it . . . this person was catapulted to just knowing what it takes for her to succeed by the sheer power of her passion, her energy and her sense of urgency.

THE SOURCE OF URGENCY

The kind of urgency I am talking about is not a momentary, transitory urge born of the moment, but something deep inside you . . . something unignorable.

It is unignorable or urgent because it is a passion arising from the core of who you are, it is about what you care and crave the most – what is most important to you, whether it is a passion . . . or an urgent need, desire or longing arising from a situation . . . or a circumstance or person that is so important to you, that you cannot . . . you will not ignore it. You *will* do something about it.

I once read that the things that compel us, that gnaw at us and won't leave us alone – our talents, our deep desires, our ideas, insights, our wisdom . . . even the things we are afraid of . . . are simply God within us asking to be expressed and realized . . . and that when we ignore or suppress those wants or needs or longings, we are really turning away from God . . . we are turning our backs on the divine part of ourselves that wants only to be expressed.

So yes – urgency is an essential part of being alive . . . an essential part of feeling really alive – what Joseph Campbell calls, *the rapture of being alive.* He says that's what all of us *really* want – to feel that we are *really alive.* He says everyone wants to feel *the rapture of being alive.* And that's what passion is . . . what a sense of urgency is.

A sense of urgency is a response to that which beckons us and calls forth the best in us. A sense of urgency is like the flow of blood inside us – continuous, nourishing and revitalizing. It is necessary for our very life – a life that is to be lived, not just endured . . . a life that is to be savored, not just worked at.

So what is a sense of urgency? Where does it come from? How do you get it?

Quite simply – a sense of urgency is what drives you. It is like rocket fuel – it ignites you with a surge of energy that gets you started . . . and sustains you thru the entire journey. It is your own inexhaustible energy supply.

The sense of urgency can be created by the sheer force of being swept up in your own passion – like Donald Trump with real estate, like Bill Gates with computers and now philanthropy, like Angelina Jolie with helping the underprivileged and disenfranchised, like my friend is, like I am about writing – then all you need to do is trust your passion, give in to it and follow where it leads you . . . unconditionally and whole-heartedly.

A sense of urgency can come from anger – anger that is channeled into success. Anger has a lot of energy and that energy can be used, can be channeled into the will to succeed.

Fear turned to desperation has a lot of energy that can be channeled into urgency – the determination to succeed.

Sometimes our sense of urgency arises from a circumstance so dire or so compelling that it creates the urgency to change it, to succeed. So many people get so lazy or complacent or comfortable, even in their misery and lack, that they can't muster the energy to feel that urgency. Or they get depressed and can't do anything, because depression has no energy at all. That's why so many people need a tragedy or trauma to do it for them . . . to mobilize the dormant energy inside them, to activate it and set it in motion, to light their fuse and set them on fire.

But you can light your own fuse . . . ignite your own fire. You can create your own source of urgency that is rooted in and motivated by something so compelling, so important to you – that you not only overcome, but completely forget about your fear, your anxiety, your depression. It will act as a great motivator and call forth the very best that is in you . . . which brings us to the next ingredient in the secret to your success – motivation.

2

THE M factOR

Motivation . . . Imagine being so motivated by something, that failure is not an option!

That's the kind of motivation I am talking about. Motivation that is yoked with urgency . . . both of which are sustained. None of these stops and starts . . . none of this beginning and then hesitating, doubting, worrying, fearing, questioning – all of which sap your energy and blur your focus.

35

All of which can actually make you dizzy from turning your head so much – from looking forward toward what you want, then snapping it backwards to look over your shoulder at your fears and what you've always had, to staring at the present, at what you see and what you are experiencing – what "the facts" are . . . to looking forward again and seeing what could happen if . . . if yes . . . if no . . . if maybe . . . if . . . if . . . if . . .

Many people feel motivated and it doesn't propel them to success. Why? Because their motivation is not urgent enough . . . not sustained enough, or because they are motivated by what they *don't* want rather than what they *do* want, so they are mired in "the facts" of the present and haunted by the ghosts of the past – so they are paralyzed by fear, or immobilized by depression or just left in a stuttering inertia of procrastination, indecision and endless planning – afraid to take the wrong step, afraid to make the wrong decision, to make any decision, when all the while – making no decision is the worst decision of all . . . and doing nothing is the most ineffective, and often destructive step they can take.

THE facts . . . aND MOTIVaTiON

Motivation not fueled by urgency, not sustained, not focusing on what you want rather than what you *don't* want, doesn't work because it has people looking backwards, always glancing over their shoulder at what *was*, so that they see what *is* and what *can be* through the filter of the past – so the future remains only what *could be* – not what *can be* – the conditional rather than the present or the future.

They think that "the facts" are reality and that "what

is", what they see, what they are experiencing, is their reality. They erroneously equate the facts of their current life and experience with who they are – and they get stuck there – not realizing that the facts of their current existence are just that – the facts about what they are presently experiencing. But facts and experiences can be changed.

I think the word "fact" is very intimidating to people. They assume a fact is like a mandate from God – something written in stone that cannot be changed. So, they believe they just have to accept it.

But facts are just statements about what "is" at that moment. Even scientific facts can be changed – and are all the time. That's the whole reason for and basis of scientific discovery, exploration and research . . . to change the facts!

Even the fact that the earth was flat was changed for a disbelieving public.

MOTiVaTiON aND DESPERaTiON

So – getting back to desperation – desperation can provide a great sense of urgent motivation depending upon how you respond to and experience your desperation. If you let it immobilize you and paralyze you with fear – if you keep looking backward at what you are afraid of or don't want, then you are not looking forward towards your success because you cannot look in two directions at the same time.

Some animals can see in both directions at the same

time, but we humans can't. So, if you are looking backward, you are not looking forward. If you are looking at what *was*, you are not looking at what *can be*. If you are looking at what you have experienced *before*, you are not looking at what you can experience *now* . . . and in the future.

I remember seeing an interview with Barbara Walters – one of the only interviews she ever gave, I think. She told how she was destined for success, how she knew she would succeed . . . because for her, failure was simply not an option.

Walters had a father who was a flamboyant night-club impresario and a serious gambler and a sister who was borderline retarded. She said she always knew she had to take care of her sister and had to support her family . . . that one day, her father would lose everything and her sister would need someone to be responsible for her care. "So, I knew I *had to* succeed," Walters said. "Failure was not an option."

I have a friend who responded quite differently to his desperation. His father had been an alcoholic and rather ineffective his whole life (what my friend called a wimp) and his mother, over-bearing. Determined not to become anything like his father, my friend spent his entire life trying *not* to become like him. He married four times, made lots of money and lost it, not once, but four times. He had incredible opportunities in his life to be successful, rich and happy, but because the focus of his life was always on what he did *not* want to be, he lost it all over and over again and again . . . and he became the one thing he did *not* want to be – a person just like his father – an alcoholic and a wimp.

Why? Because his motivation was always, without fail, what he did *not* want . . . not what he *did* want. His focus was always on the past, rather than on the present and the future.

When our motivation is a negative one, we will always get the very thing we do *not* want. Why? Because that's where our attention is. That's what our focus is on. That's where we put the most energy . . . and God, the Universe, luck, synchronicity – whatever you want to call it – responds to that as if it is what we want . . . and gives it to us.

It seems that God, the Universe, the One, the All, the Great Spirit (the ancient Greeks called it the Logos) . . . whatever you want to call that *something greater than us* that is within all things and governs the universe, does not seem to understand and respond to the word *not,* or *never*, or *don't*, or *no* . . . it just hears and responds to the nouns we concentrate on and gives us those things we focus on.

That's one of the main reasons why so many people who are overweight can't and don't lose weight. They are always focusing on food, which they feel they can't eat; on pounds which they don't want; on weight which they want to lose; and on clothes which they can't buy or fit into. So, that's what they get more of . . . that's what their lives and experience center around and consist

41

of – the things they can't have, don't want and can't do.

Motivation and the Status Quo

I once read a quote that said, "It's never too late to become what you might have been." Sounds obvious and simple, but I find that those are often the most profound and easily overlooked insights.

So many people give up before they even try because they convince themselves that they are either too fat, too poor, too uneducated, too old . . . too whatever, to do what they want to do. Personally, I think that's a cop-out – it's their safety net, their "acceptable excuse" to themselves and others for not even trying, for not risking failure, for not risking success, for being lazy, for investing in the status quo at the same time they are complaining about it.

The status quo, even when it is something we don't want, something undesirable, uncomfortable or embarrassing . . . even when it goes against everything we want, believe in and are . . . is still often more compelling than a change, any change, no matter how exciting and desirable that change may be.

We human beings are funny. We want everything to change, but nothing to change. We want our financial situation to change, our love life to change, our family life to be different . . . we want a whole new life, yet we hold on fiercely and tenaciously to everything just as it is. We don't want to change our friends, we don't want to change the way we do things, we don't want to change what we do, who we see, how we spend each day . . . but . . . we want to be richer, happier and more successful than we are now.

I know it sounds crazy . . . and obvious . . . but most people really do hang on to the status quo while wishing everything were different.

THE TIPPING POINT

And maybe that's the key . . . we can't *wish* things were different, we can't *want* things to be different. It has to be something stronger than just wishing and wanting. Desire alone is not enough. That desire – that motivation – has to be fueled by passion, urgency and determination. Something has to be decided upon . . . and something has to be committed to.

And these are not easy things to do. It's easy to

45

feel passion in the moment, to feel a sense of urgency for a day, to be determined at the outset of something. But deciding to *do* something – really making a firm, unwavering decision – a commitment – is very difficult for most people. Most people are so unused to making a decision about anything in their lives, that they don't even really know what it feels like to make a categorical decision – one from which there is no turning back

People are so used to being vague and non-committal that they don't understand the power that making a firm decision wields. Or maybe they do . . . and that power is so scary, that it stops them from making a decision, any decision, because then they know they will *have to* do it.

But that's the kind of motivation I am talking about – motivation as commitment, motivation as urgency, motivation as success being the only option. Scary? Yes. But also exciting, thrilling, energizing, liberating, revitalizing . . . and yes, a doorway into feeling *the rapture of being alive.* Because when you care about something so much that you are willing to do whatever it takes, to never stop, never give in, never falter; it empowers and emboldens you, so that you *can do* whatever it takes to never stop, never give in, never falter.

It frees up all that energy that is being sapped and dissipated in indecisiveness, fear, wavering and procrastination. All of these use up enormous amounts of energy and produce no results . . . no satisfaction.

So what is that tipping point – the point at which your motivation becomes something you no longer think about, dream of, wish for and pray about? The point at which you are set in motion and move only forward from that point on . . . you look and see only ahead of you and not behind?

It's different for everyone. Sometimes it comes in a flash; sometimes it takes years . . . even a lifetime. Unfortunately, for many people, that tipping point comes as a result of tragedy, trauma or illness that wakes them up . . . literally, like an alarm clock announcing . . . wake up, it's time, do something, do it now, don't wait.

Maybe, that's what it takes to give them the energy they need, to do what they want to do or what they have to do. It takes a huge amount of energy to set yourself in motion, starting from a stationary position. And tragedy, trauma or illness often provide that lift-off that activates people's "on" button.

A friend of mine was a workaholic, depressed for most of her life (depression is often just anger turned inward, so it has no energy), non-communicative and emotionally unavailable, even to those she loved. Her life consisted of going to work, coming home, eating and lying on the sofa watching TV until she fell asleep. She had no social life, no fun, was way overweight, and dressed abysmally, which reflected how she felt about and saw herself.

Then, she found out she had cancer. Well fortunately, she breezed through that like a thoroughbred . . .

almost as if she had been expecting it . . . as if she had been waiting for it, for something to turn her on. She went into high gear after her surgery – she quit her job, began exercising and lost weight, bought new clothes, made friends, started travelling, and began to fill up her social calendar so that she barely had a free minute.

After over forty years of being lethargic, bored, practically comatose her entire adult life . . . she came alive. Why? Because she thought she was going to die . . . so she had an urgent, unignorable motivation that propelled her into now and helped her create a future. It was so powerful, that she never looked back, only forward . . . saw only *now*, what can I do *now*, what do I want *now* and every day of my life . . . and she was motivated to get it, do it, be it, have it.

In the film *Oh God II*, God (George Burns) enlists the help of a little girl to get his message out to people. When he does so, he tells her she has one week to do it. "One week!" she complains. And then he gives her some of the most valuable advice I've ever heard . . . again . . . it is both simple and obvious, and therefore, easily overlooked. "Nothing ever gets done without a deadline," God says. I try to remember that . . . and try to set my own deadlines before life sets them for me.

CREATING URGENT MOTIVATION

If you have a passion, a talent that won't leave you alone, a love of something that makes your blood rush at the mere thought of doing it, being it, having it . . . then you are fortunate . . . blessed, even.

If you are experiencing or have experienced a wake-up call in the form of tragedy, trauma or illness . . . then you have the choice of responding to it with paralyzing fear or sadness . . . or as a call to life . . . a call to wake up and do it, do it now, don't wait – whatever *it* is.

But you can also *create* your own motivation infused with urgency, because one without the other will not work. They must be yoked together . . . and they must be sustained.

Imagine, like the young Barbara Walters, you have a father who you know is going to lose everything and a sister who is helpless and you are the only one who can take care of her. What will (not would) you do?

Imagine you are about to lose your children in a custody case unless you make a million dollars in one year. Will you do it? I guarantee you will find a way to make it happen so you can keep your children with you. (Remember, the urgent motivation must always be positive.)

Imagine that you are being chased by people who want to kill you or that someone you love is stranded on the other side of a gorge and will die if you don't get there and rescue them in three days or that you are being given a million dollars on only one condition – you conquer your biggest fear. Will you do it? Will you walk that rope bridge suspended over the gorge, even though you are terrified of heights, or climb that mountain peak, or go to the bottom of that deep, dark cavernous cave, even though you are obsessively claustrophobic?

There have been films about such circumstances, books written about such hypothetical situations . . . so why not *create your own real hypothetical* (I know that sounds like an oxymoron) *urgent motivation*? Why wait for a tragedy, trauma or illness to force you to? Why wait for life to intercede? Do it yourself . . . and on your own terms. Create your own urgent situation – your own unignorable motivation. Do it now. Decide what you want . . . no, not what you *want* . . . decide what you are *going to have, be or do* . . . and then set the deadline . . . and do it.

Create the motivation that compels you – something bigger than just you, more specific than money or happiness – something so important that you cannot, you will not ignore it, let it down or fail . . . because failure is not an option. Create a motivation so important, that success is the only option. And then . . . act as though you cannot fail . . . and you will become infused with a power, an energy, an "unstoppableness" that move you toward a success that is certain.

3

THE Mz factor

So many people get excited about something, motivated by something, even begin it, talk about it, plan for it . . . and then fizzle out. They never do it, never complete it.

They lose their energy, their focus, interest . . . They lose their momentum – the third key to unlocking the secret of your success.

Momentum – the forward continuous movement

toward what you want – goes all the way back to the beginning . . . making a decision – a firm, unwavering decision from which you cannot, you will not deviate.

Such a decision is made when and because it is infused with a sense of urgency . . . a sense, not a feeling. Feelings are fleeting and fickle; they lack the power of a commitment so they cannot be sustained, can't be trusted not to waver or change. But a *sense* of urgency is pervasive. It courses through us so that every cell in our body is vibrating with this urgency.

It is this urgency that creates momentum. But creating momentum is the easy part . . . sustaining it is the hard part. It's easy to begin things, especially when you are caught in the grip of that adrenalin rush – the urgent call to action. But sustaining that level of enthusiasm, that level of commitment and energy requires that ineffable *something* that only comes from passion (which can come from desperation, anger, love, creativity) . . . from combining your sense of urgency with a positive motivation that is so much bigger than you are, that you dare not fail or stop or waver.

And you can sustain this momentum because you have a goal in sight. Your motivation is specific, clear, defined . . . and your deadline is set – all of which make the urgency manageable and the sustained momentum possible.

MOMENTUM AND INERTIA

What is inertia? People erroneously associate inertia with inactivity and lack of movement. Not so. Inertia is "a property of matter by which it remains at rest or *in uniform motion* in the same straight line *unless acted upon by some external force.*"

What does that mean? Quite simply, it means that an object at rest will stay at rest . . . and . . . an *object in motion will stay in motion*, unless acted upon by some external force.   So inertia refers to movement as well as stasis.

When we talk about inertia, we refer to *the force of inertia*. So inertia has both energy and movement . . . It *is* a force and it *does* have power.

Understanding this is essential for creating and sustaining momentum . . . for understanding, appreciating and harnessing the power of momentum – the force of a moving object.

Most people are creating their initial momentum from zero . . . or less than zero.   They are coming from despair, depression, immobilizing fear, boredom, lethargy, hopelessness, laziness, procrastination – all of which are huge energy drains so the person's storehouse of energy and resources is literally less than zero.

So when they reach their *tipping point* and their sense of urgency kicks in and their positive motivation becomes all-consuming, they experience a real rush – a high.   That initial surge of energy, like a shot of adrenalin, wears off though . . . and they can *crash* or stop, and then they have to start all over again, from zero or less than.   If they do this enough, they will eventually lose hope, get exhausted, or just give up.

And they wind up giving up only because they don't understand *the principle of inertia – that once you are in motion, you have to stay in motion.* When Lao Tzu or Deepak Chopra or anyone talks about doing things with effortless ease, they are speaking of inertia as one of the components of that ease.   Once you create the movement, the flow . . . you will accomplish things much more easily and quickly if you continue that flow rather than if you stop and start, because then each time, you need to create a new movement out of non-movement all over again.

That's why so many people get discouraged after the initial surge of excitement and flurry of activity – they stop, they hesitate, they begin to doubt, they over-analyze, they plan too much and too long, they perfect and over-perfect, they line their ducks up over and over and over again *ad nauseum* until even *they* are bored with what they are doing . . . bored with the very same thing that originally set their heart on fire at the mere thought of it.

But when you are driven by a positive motivation that is bigger than just you, and when that motivation is fueled by a sense of urgency, sustaining your momentum becomes infinitely simpler . . . and finding and doing what you need to sustain that motivation becomes exponentially easier.

The River of Momentum

"We all need to be reminded of the obvious." Why? Just because it's so obvious, we overlook it; we take it for granted.

Rivers have tributaries to feed them. If rivers had to depend solely on their own water supply, many of them would dry up and stop running.

It's the same with people. We all need that occasional or regular "shot in the arm" from a coach, a friend, a book, a program, a course . . . We are social creatures. We have complex brains, expansive psyches and soaring spirits that need to be in touch with other human beings to explore, confirm, affirm, inspire, enlighten, empower . . . or just to be there and listen.

So, during your progress on your road to success, when you feel yourself about to falter, beginning to doubt, in danger of hesitating or looking back . . . when you feel yourself in danger of stopping the momentum you have created, the force of inertia that you have set in motion . . . immediately grab a book, call a friend, contact your coach, turn on an inspirational program . . . do anything you have to, to lift yourself up out of that snare, to continue staying in motion, staying enthused, staying on course with your sense of urgency and positive motivation in tact . . . calling to you, driving you.

It is not a sign of weakness, but a sign of strength and an act of wisdom to reach out when you need help to stay motivated and on course. You have worked too hard to create the momentum you already have going, to jeopardize it with pride and inaction. And what you are moving toward is too important for you to retreat into old habits of lethargy, doubt, procrastination or pride.

So do it and do it immediately. It doesn't have to be some long drawn out thing, just constant, or on an as need basis, so it is always feeding your energy flow, like the tributaries feeding a river, so it doesn't stop and stagnate. Stagnant water develops all sorts of impurities . . . and stagnant energy will do the same, hampering your efforts to begin again – to re-establish your momentum – if you wait too long or stop too often.

THE fORCE Of a MOViNG OBJECT

Momentum is defined as "the force of a moving object." But what does *moving* mean? Does it mean that you must be in constant motion, never stopping, never resting, always on the go? Sounds exhausting.

In the physical world, moving does mean "in motion." But in the metaphysical world – the world beyond the physical in which urgency and motivation work synergistically to create and sustain momentum – moving can actually mean standing still.

How can movement and standing still be the same thing? Because there are different kinds of movement, different degrees, different arenas. Sometimes we move very little on the outside, while making great progress on the inside. That's actually the basis of many minimalist arts and Eastern exercises like Tai Chi and Qi Gong, for example . . . or Trager or Network Chiropractic. You move very little to accomplish a lot.

Sometimes you barely move or don't even move at all. Sometimes you are processing, assimilating . . . and need to be still and patient . . . and trust.

I find that trust and patience are a large part of sustaining my momentum. If I stay in constant motion, if I am continually busy and *doing*, I exhaust and deplete myself. I get enervated because I can only maintain that level of activity for so long without burning out.

So your sustained momentum includes periods of stillness during which you process what you need to; you replenish and revitalize, you allow . . . whatever it is you need to allow to happen, to come to you, to ripen, to appear.

And then you harness the power of that movement inside of you and fold it back into the force of the moving object – you. You weave it into your momentum, intensifying its effectivensss with a boldness and a stillness that is authentically you.

SILENCE AND MOMENTUM

Yes, momentum even has an audio component. Silence is a powerful mover. It intensifies things. It clarifies things. It lets you hear things you wouldn't hear without the silence.

Silence allows your momentum to crescendo, to peak and valley like a wave – always in motion, but modulated. And modulation is so important for being able to sustain your momentum because without modulation, the intensity, the level, the amount of your momentum would be nearly impossible to sustain at a constant level . . . and ultimately, would become tedious, monotonous, unproductive and overwhelming.

In addition to your personal moments of silence, it is also important not to talk a lot about what you are doing and why you are doing it. Don't talk about it a lot or tell people about it. By doing so, you dissipate the energy and actually slow down and interfere with the momentum. Every time you stop to answer someone's question, or tell somebody something about it, you side-track, like getting off the main road onto a winding side road that takes you way out of your way.

Plus you open up that laser sharp focus and intensity of your urgent motivation to the energy, the doubts, the questions, the jealousy, the unasked for input, advice and thoughts of everyone to whom you speak about it. You are inviting in the sluggard as well as the enthusiast, the cynic as well as the idealist. Better to contain and control the input, the intensity, the focus by not spreading the word around . . . not spending your time and energy talking about what you are doing . . . at least, not while you are in the process of initially creating your success.

THE QUIET POWER OF MOMENTUM

I recently saw a story on TV about a man who was broke, suicidal and had given up on life and himself. He had a troubled adolescence and began dealing drugs. When he fell in love, his wife also got involved and was killed on a drug deal gone bad.

Blaming himself for her death, he gave their daughter up for adoption and proceeded to spiral down deeper and deeper into depression until an opportunity arose for him to go to Africa to help out some orphans in war-torn Congo. A self-taught carpenter, he went to help out with the construction of a hospital, but found he received more help there than he ever gave. There, he found a passion . . . he found a sense of urgency . . . he found a positive motivation bigger than himself . . . and he created a momentum that he sustains by staying there and continuing to build things for the orphans . . . continuing to build a life for them and a life for himself . . . with a quiet, but powerful sustained determination.

This man is a success . . . quietly doing his thing with a sense of urgency that involves no flourishes, no announcements; a motivation that is bigger than himself; and a momentum that is sustained by his vision of and involvement in both . . . sustained by his love for what he is doing, a sense of purpose, and a feeling of profound happiness . . . knowing that his life matters.

4

UMM

I think it's interesting that *UMM* is so reminiscent of *OM* . . . both of which help us ignite and sustain something very important – the former . . . motivation, the latter . . . inspiration. Both are powerful, but *UMM* originates from within us and is fueled by our organic, authentic selves. It can be helped by things outside of us, but does not need them.

UMM, like the holy sound of *OM*, is self-contained

– like a hologram, the whole is contained in the parts. So, although we have talked about urgency, motivation and momentum separately . . . they cannot be separated. They weave in and out of each other like a living tapestry – synergistic and self-contained . . . something more than the sum of its parts.

I remember studying Chemistry in High School and learning the difference between a mixture and a compound – a lesson I have found very useful throughout my life. A lesson that helps me understand that sometimes 1 + 1 does not equal 2, but something *other* than 2.

Quite simply (to refresh your memory, in case you have forgotten your High School Chemistry), a mixture is the substance that results from mixing two or more elements that remain separate and their own unique selves. They do not merge into one another. They do not dissolve and coalesce, like the elements in a compound do. A compound is the joining of two or more substances to form a third substance. The original elements lose their own individual identities to form a third entity, something that can no longer be easily separated into its component parts – like hydrogen and oxygen to form water, or H_2O.

That's what happens when you combine urgency, motivation and momentum – they become something more than just the sum of their parts. The synergy between them creates something powerful, a force that is unstoppable and a will that is unwavering and assured of its goal.

LOVE AND THE UMM FACTOR

I thought of including this in the chapter on urgency . . . calling it *Love and Urgency*, but it's more than that. Love is the universalizing element that enables everyone to understand the synergy between the three elements that make up your *UMM* Factor.

Not everyone has a passion; not all people's fear intensifies enough to lift them out of their paralysis and immobility into a desperation that catapults them into action and motion; not everyone can or is ready to channel their anger into positive energy . . . but everyone has felt, been moved by, craved and been sustained by love.

Love is the one thing that can translate the three elements of the *UMM* Factor into a universal language that everyone can understand, relate to, and see themselves compelled by. Love is the common denominator that can activate everybody's "on" switch . . . and set them in motion.

A friend of mine, whose spirit had been destroyed and her *joie de vivre* extinguished in an abusive first marriage, was pretty much numb her whole adult life. Her anger, which usually has a lot of energy when it is directed outward, turned inward to become a lifelong immobilizing depression . . . so that, even with those she loved dearly – her husband, her children and her family – she was unable to muster any energy to show or express that love.

She wasn't even able to muster the energy to do *any* living . . . and she pretty much just went to work, watched television, slept a lot and was angry at just about everyone, no matter what they did or didn't do. She was even angry at her daughter for moving to and building a life in a city that was hundreds of miles away. My friend was intransigent, inflexible, negative, and as emotionally dead and hard as a rock.

All that changed when her daughter gave birth to her first grandchild. Overcome with such love for her grandson, her desperate fear that she would not be a part of his life because she lived so far away from him, turned to determination to be a part of his life at any cost . . . and my friend, who never made any decisions about anything; who never took any action on anything; who felt and acted like a helpless victim her entire adult life . . . decided that her grandson was too important to her and that, no matter what she had to do, she was going to be an important, integral part of his life from that moment on.

He was so important to her, that she decided she was not going to miss any of the years . . . any precious time with him from the time he was born until the time he grew up. And so, this person – who was bored, inactive, a stay at homer, a sleeper and a television watcher, a person who was obsessed with money and security and worked and worked and worked to assuage and satisfy those obsessions, began taking time off from work, long weekends, and doing whatever she had to in order to spend time with her grandson.

She would fly up for a day or a weekend; she would fly up and get him and bring him back down to her for a week and then fly up again to bring him home and then turn around and fly right back home again. This continued until her daughter had another child . . . after which my friend intensified and increased the time she spent with both of them . . . no matter what she had to do to make it happen. This has gone on for fifteen years now, and she has continued to be as much a part of her grandchildren's lives as if she lived close by.

Her *UMM* Factor was very high and was therefore unignorable. She had to do something about it in order to be able to live with herself, to look in the mirror, to wake up each morning and face each day. Nothing was more important to her than her grandchildren.

WHaT iS YOUR UMM factor?

You need to know this in order to succeed. But success means different things to different people – it can mean lots of money, fame, prestige, travel, material possessions, creative accomplishments . . . or simple things like milk or spending time with your grandchildren.

So, urgency and motivation don't have to be over-whelming or fierce or even about grand things . . . they just have to be compelling. A motivation becomes urgent

73

because something is so important to you that you cannot, you will not ignore its call . . . or because there is a deadline.

Time is our most precious commodity. Once it's gone, it's gone. We cannot buy it back, no matter how much money we have. So the finiteness of time forces us to prioritize . . . and often compels us to take action.

What is so important to you that you cannot . . . you will not ignore its call? What do you feel the finiteness of time closing in on . . . its panting tongue lapping up behind it?

THE PaNTiN9 TON9uE Of TiME

Racing with time can wear you out. It's a race you can't win – a game you can only play, not to win . . . but to enjoy.

My best friend was in a relationship with someone for sixteen years. He was brilliant, talented, creative, extraordinarily smart, sharp and intelligent – he had street smarts, real life smarts and book smarts. He had it all and could have done or been anything he wanted . . . and succeeded.

But he was haunted by memories of watching all his family's possessions being taken from them when he was a little boy, by the fear of never knowing when they would lose everything because of a father who gambled, so he was driven by the need to make money, the compulsion to succeed in business, to create financial security for himself and his family.

So, he channeled his fear and anger into the will to succeed, the determination to live well and securely; but there was always a part of him that went unsatisfied . . . no, not unsatisfied . . . it was frustrated. He was artistic, talented, creative, brilliant . . . and he was putting all his energy into making money and doing things he did not love or care about – things that would bring him security and money, which he discovered were not enough to make him happy . . . not enough to make him feel like a success.

Then he and my friend broke up and he threw himself even further into work . . . courting a high paying job in New York, which he had always avoided because of its freneticism and high energy demands. And after two years, just when he was being offered the position he had been coveting and lusting after, he found out that my friend's uncle – a beloved older artist she had introduced him to who became his mentor, a friend and a brilliant, inspiring, devoted artist – had died.

This unexpected loss jolted him so, that he turned down the job and began searching . . . searching for that part of himself that had gotten lost . . . searching for what he wanted to do . . . searching for that which he loved and wanted to spend his precious time left on earth doing. The loss of someone iconic and timeless to him made him realize the finiteness of time . . . and created in him, a new sense of urgency and positive motivation.

As a way of honoring and celebrating the life of this timeless icon who had meant so much to him, who had given so much to life, he embarked on a mission to become who he might have been had he not been driven to make money and succeed in business at all costs. And he did. He became a photographer – a very good one . . . a very successful one . . . and a very happy one.

He transformed one sense of urgency and positive motivation that was bigger than him into another. He shifted his *UMM* Factor from the world of business to the world of art. He exchanged security for happiness . . . both of which have brought him a high degree of success because the *UMM* Factor has always been what drives him, what fuels his actions and what sustains his momentum.

THE UMM factor aND Success

So your *UMM* Factor is not a fixed thing . . . it can change and grow as you do.

It's all energy – so you can take that same energy that you have been putting into fear, desperation, anger, anxiety, worrying, etc. – and channel it into a positive urgency . . . just like my friend's ex-boyfriend did.

Winston Churchill is reputed to have said that, "Success is the ability to go from one failure to another without any loss of enthusiasm." So perhaps he and I are saying the same thing, just using different words. You have got to sustain your powerful determination if you want to succeed.

Churchill was once called upon to give a commencement speech at a university graduation and the story goes that he strode slowly up to the stage, placed both hands on the podium, and cordially greeted everyone, "Friends, family, faculty, and all you young graduates," and then he proceeded on to his speech . . . "Never . . . Never . . . Never . . . Never . . . Never give up!"

And then he turned and walked back to his seat.

That is probably the shortest commencement address ever given . . . but perhaps, the most effective.

So, for your commencement – for whatever it is that you are beginning, graduating to or initiating – create a strong, unwavering *UMM* Factor with a sustained sense of urgency that is fueled by a sustained positive motivation that is kept in motion by sustained momentum . . . and you *will* succeed.

5

YOUR UMM factor

Whether you are motivated to accomplish grand things . . . or just buy milk or spend time with your grand-children, do not underestimate the power of a specific, positive motivation. It's always in the specifics that the power lies. I always teach people that when I am coaching them in writing. It's in the details that you capture your audience and tell your story . . . in the specifics that you etch your characters.

And so it is with all of life . . . it is the specifics that capture our attention, the small or private things sometimes that ultimately motivate us – like milk. But it is always something that calls to us, not something that pushes us away.

Last year, I saw an interesting experiment chronicled on one of the TV news magazine shows to determine the comparative power of positive and negative motivation. In a small town, a group of overweight people was divided into two smaller groups. Each person in both groups had his or her photo taken at the outset . . . naked! (Remember, these were people who were seriously overweight . . . and people living in a really small town where everyone knew everyone else!) One team was told that as they lost weight in incremental amounts, they would be given fabulous specific rewards and prizes. The other team was told that if they did not lose as much weight as the other, their nude *before* photos would be displayed on the big screen at the local football field.

Wow! I am a firm believer in positive motivation, but even I had my doubts about the outcome of this! The fear, shame, humiliation and sheer terror of having the nude photo of your obese, fat, overweight body displayed on a big screen at the football field for everyone in your small town to see, certainly seemed like it would be a powerful motivator.

Well, it was . . . but not powerful enough. The team that was reinforced with specific, incremental positive rewards lost more weight than the team that was living under the threat of having their pre-diet naked bodies exposed and

THE UMM factor

displayed in front of everyone. As unbelievable as that may sound to you . . . the positive motivation was stronger and more effective than the negative fear of failure. Why?

Because of performance . . . because you cannot look back in fear and forward in anticipation at the same time . . . because the fear was an energy drain, while the positive motivation was an energy booster. And in order to perform at peak, no matter what you are doing, you must be fueled by the forward moving, positive energy that empowers and energizes you to succeed. Success is the result of the culmination of something, not the avoidance of something.

And the incremental, continuous rewards through-out the program helped the winning team maintain their momentum, their energy level, their motivation. It harnessed the force of inertia to keep them in motion, whereas the other team did not have that advantage.

So, although there is no one path to success, no one way to succeed . . . there are three qualities you can cultivate that can promote, and even guarantee your success . . . 3 keys to unlocking the secrets to your success . . .

URGENCY

MOTIVATION

MOMENTUM

THE UMM factor

. . . .

THE UMM factOR

· ·

The 3 Things You Need In Order To Succeed

· · · · · · · · · · · · ·

Create a sense of *urgency* and sustain it.

Drive your urgency with a positive *motivation* that is
bigger than you
and calls forth the best in you.

Once in motion, stay in motion and sustain that power of
inertia that gives you
momentum – the force of a moving object.

———————————

Then savor every step of the way and EnjOy!

DO THESE 3 THINGS — AND YOU <u>WILL</u> SUCCEED . . . guaranteed!

Develop a Sense of URGENCY

A sense of urgency is what drives you.

A sense of urgency mobilizes all your energy so you can accomplish things with effortless ease.

A sense of urgency creates a deadline so your urgency is manageable and effective.

A sense of urgency is like the organizing principle, creating order out of chaos – like a kaleidoscope creating a beautiful pattern out of myriad pieces of broken glass.

Find Your Positive MOTIVATION

Motivation yoked with urgency enables you to accomplish things in record time with almost superhuman capabilities.

Motivation yoked with urgency eliminates all doubts, fears, hesitations, procrastination, all conditions and hypothetical "ifs" and replaces them with yes I can . . . yes I will . . . yes I am.

A positive motivation that is bigger than you are, calls forth the best in you.

An urgent, positive motivation that is bigger than you are, laser sharpens your focus so it is clear and defined.

Create a Sustained MOMENTUM

Momentum is the forward continuous movement toward what you want.

Momentum is the force of a moving object.

Momentum is fueled by a sense of urgency and a powerful, positive motivation that is bigger than you are.

Momentum is powered by the force of inertia.

MOTiVaTiONaL QUOTES

Success is the only option.

Failure is not an option.

Act as though you cannot fail.

Passion makes you unstoppable.

A sense of urgency takes the risk *out of* risk.

Milk . . . you are fighting for milk.

An object in motion will stay in motion.

The force of inertia sustains your momentum.

You are always motivated by what you *do* want.

Nothing ever gets done without a deadline.

Passion is power.

Create your own *real hypothetical* urgent motivation.

Your success is guaranteed.

Your life matters . . . and you were born to succeed. Your success is guaranteed if you will open up to, cultivate, and harness the power of a sense of urgency, a positive motivation that is bigger than you are, and a sustained momentum – the three keys to unlocking the secret to your success.

.

6

TUNiNg iN

That probably sounds weird to you – telling you to tune into your sense of urgency . . . to become aware of it. "How can you not be aware of it?" you are probably wondering.

Easy . . . most of us have gotten so used to living with stress, "burning the candle at both ends" (afraid to do something and afraid not to); we are so used to living under pressure and are often addicted to, and have become comfortable with the drama that urgency creates, that we no longer experience the urgency as urgent. Our high level stress and pressured lives take the urgency out of urgency; they camouflage it so that we often experience our urgency as ordinary, everyday stress which we have come to accept, expect and live with.

We must put the urgency back into urgency so that we respond to it willingly and proactively . . . rather than waiting for illness, tragedy, trauma or dire circumstances to come along and force us to react.

So, a high *UMM* Factor will guarantee your success when you do one thing – tune into it.

Tuning into your sense of urgency and motivation will activate the synergy between them and set you in motion . . . then all you need to do is harness the power of inertia to stay in motion and sustain your momentum.

If you care deeply about something and still can't seem to muster the energy (either because of laziness, complacency, or just plain habit) and that sense of urgency to propel you into action . . . then create it, before life does it for you. Create something so compelling that it gets you up in the morning, it takes the work out of work, it puts the urgency back into urgency and sets you in motion so you don't stop until you have it, do it, are it.

Create it . . . and then let it move you to commit . . . So everything inside of you . . . and outside of you . . . is mobilized to help you fulfill that commitment – to help you succeed.

The moment one definitely commits oneself,
then providence moves too.
All sorts of things occur to help one
that would never otherwise have occurred.
A whole stream of events issues from
the decisions, raising in one's favor all manner of
unforeseen incidents and meetings and material
assistance which no man could have dreamed
would have come his way.

Johann Wolfgang von Goethe

ABOUT THE AUTHOR

Madeleine Kay is the Best Selling Author of *Living Serendipitously* and *Serendipitously Rich*. Adventurist, unconventional success and motivational coach . . . and maverick entrepreneur, she has been featured in *Who's Who of American Women* and *Who's Who in the World.*

She speaks four languages, has been a resident

of three continents, been a university instructor and international fashion model on two continents, ran her own advertising and marketing agency, wrote commentaries for the CBS affiliate in Miami and was even an actor in film, television and a music video.

Considered America's leading expert on *serendipity*, she combines the wisdom, passion and playfulness of serendipity sprinkled with her own unique brand of practical, down-to-earth common sense to help people get, claim and enjoy all the joy and riches they desire.

BOOKS BY MADELEINE KAY

Living Serendipitously . . . keeping the wonder alive

A lively and joyful read, *Living Serendipitously* gets you to be an *active dreamer*, living your dreams, not just thinking about them. It captures the joyful essence of "the art of living" and shows you how to feel deliciously *alive,* vibrant and happy every day of your life . . . no matter what your circumstances. Einstein said, "There are only two ways to live your life – as though nothing is a miracle or as though everything is a miracle." *Living Serendipitously* aligns us with the *everything.*
(visit www.livingserendipitously.com or your favorite bookstore or online store)

Living with Outrageous Joy

Joy is contagious . . . joy is revitalizing . . . joy is what every one of us wants to feel more of in our lives every single day. This delightful little gift book will re-ignite that feeling of joy in your life and your passion for living. Playfully inspiring and motivating, *Living with Outrageous Joy* will delight and revitalize you. It will open you up to the joy and adventure of living your life to the fullest every single day . . . unleashing in you that feeling of *aliveness* that so many of us are longing to feel.
(visit www.madeleinekay.com or your favorite bookstore or online store)

Serendipitously Rich . . .
How to Get Delightfully, Delectably, Deliciously Rich
(or anything else you want) in 7 <u>Ridiculously</u> Easy Steps

Changing *if* I am rich to *when* I am rich has never been simpler . . . or more fun. Refreshingly original and excitingly new, *Serendipitously Rich* will not only motivate and inspire you – it will activate your "on" switch, your "go" switch, your whatever it is that makes you *do* something switch, so you can stop struggling and start getting rich (and everything else you want) . . . with effortless ease and unmitigated joy.
(visit <u>www.serendipitouslyrich.com</u> or your favorite bookstore or online store)

The 7 Secrets to Living with Joy and Riches

Joy and riches . . . Isn't that what everyone wants? This charming gift book will delight and inspire you . . . and help you bring more of both into your life. You will find yourself picking it up over and over again, throughout the day, to savor the deliciously compelling exuberance and wisdom you will find on every page. A fabulous gift for everyone you know . . . and an indispensable personal companion.
(visit <u>www.madeleinekay.com</u> or your favorite bookstore or online store)

The 12 Myths About Money

Money! We all need it . . . Everyone wants it . . . Nobody wants to admit they care about it . . . And we all wish we had more – Lots more! So why isn't everyone rich? *The 12 Myths About Money* reveals your hidden core beliefs that are keeping you from becoming rich, and shows you how to instantly replace them with new beliefs that will empower you to think and act like "The Rich" do. The simple *action plan* helps you begin making these new beliefs work for you – now . . . so you can get, claim and enjoy all the riches you desire.

(Currently available as an e-book and soon available as paperback. Visit www.madeleinekay.com)

Coming Soon

Internet Success – 12 Secrets Revealed

Focused on what is simple, fast, easy and inexpensive, this book will help you get started creating your own internet business with little or no technical knowledge or know-how and with little or no money. Rather than talking about the most obvious or the very complicated, technical or expensive ways to succeed on the internet (on which there are plenty of books), this book shares with you – as simply and succinctly as possible – twelve really simple, easy-to-do, inexpensive secrets about creating success online, so you don't have to spend years learning it all.

How Will I Ever Get Over My Happy Childhood
(Stories)

This collection of first person stories is original, refreshing and deliciously compelling with its zany characters and stories that will touch and delight you . . . and that you will long remember. These stories will make you laugh, make you cry, make you feel the sheer joy of being a human being as you realize how crazy and wonderful . . . how absurdly, and sometimes hilariously imperfect we are. Exquisitely written, these stories will take you through the whole gamut of emotions and quite literally, "knock your socks off" – so grab onto your hats and enjoy the ride!

. . . .

Madeleine Kay is the Founder of the *Serendipity Day Holiday*, celebrated August 18th. You can learn about this exciting new event and how to live serendipitously all year long at . . . www.facebook.com/serendipityday

Browse *serendipity* wearables, carryables, and other "fun stuff" at *The Serendipity Shoppe* at . . . www.cafepress.com/serendip_shoppe

Receive a ***FREE*** copy of *The Serendipity Handbook* at . . . www.serendipitydayholiday.com

Also receive a ***FREE*** online *7 Myths About Money* E-course and E-book at . . . www.madeleinekay.com

. . . .

. . . .

Follow Madeleine's blog online at . . .
www.madeleinekaylive.com

For personal one-on-one mentoring or coaching, contact
Madeleine at . . . www.madeleinekay.com

. . . .

NOTES

NOTES

NOTES

NOTES